Émilie Penou

21 DAYS TO LEARN TO
crochet

× *daily practice* ×

× *step-by-step instructions* ×

× *7 projects* ×

stashBOOKS
an imprint of C&T Publishing

21 Days to Learn to Crochet

First published in the United States in 2025 by Stash Books, an imprint of C&T Publishing, Inc., P.O. Box 1456, Lafayette, CA 94549

21 jours pour apprendre le crochet © 2023 by Éditions Marie Claire - Société d'Information et de Créations (SIC)

This edition of "*21 jours pour apprendre le crochet*" first published in France by Éditions Marie Claire in 2023 is published by arrangement with SIC – Société d'Information et de Créations.

PUBLISHER: Amy Barrett-Daffin

CREATIVE DIRECTOR: Gailen Runge

SENIOR EDITOR: Roxane Cerda

ENGLISH LANGUAGE COVER DESIGNER AND LAYOUT ARTIST: April Mostek

ENGLISH TRANSLATION: Kristy Darling Finder

PRODUCTION COORDINATORS: Casey Dukes and Zinnia Heinzmann

PROJECTS AND EXPLANATIONS: Émilie Penou

EDITING AND REVISION: Véronique Blanc

PHOTOGRAPHY: Fabrice Basse, page 11 photo by puha dorin/Shutterstock.com,
page 12 photo by Africa Studio/Shutterstock.com

GRAPHIC ICONS: Crochet hook icon on page 11 by Black Silhouette/Shutterstock.com,
yarn weight icon on page 11 from Craft Yarn Council's YarnStandards.com

GRAPHIC DESIGN AND LAYOUT: Nord Compo

COVER: Claire Morel Fatio

All rights reserved. No part of this work covered by the copyright hereon may be used in any form or reproduced by any means—graphic, electronic, or mechanical, including photocopying, recording, taping, or information storage and retrieval systems—without written permission from the publisher. These designs may be used to make items for personal use only and may not be used for the purpose of personal profit. Items created to benefit nonprofit groups, or that will be publicly displayed, must be conspicuously labeled with the following credit: "Designs copyright © 2023 by Éditions Marie Claire - Société d'Information et de Créations (SIC) from the book *21 Days to Learn to Crochet* from C&T Publishing, Inc." Permission for all other purposes must be requested in writing from C&T Publishing, Inc.

Attention Teachers: C&T Publishing, Inc., encourages the use of our books as texts for teaching. You can find lesson plans for many of our titles at ctpub.com or contact us at ctinfo@ctpub.com.

We take great care to ensure that the information included in our products is accurate and presented in good faith, but no warranty is provided, nor are results guaranteed. Having no control over the choices of materials or procedures used, neither the author nor C&T Publishing, Inc., shall have any liability to any person or entity with respect to any loss or damage caused directly or indirectly by the information contained in this book. For your convenience, we post an up-to-date listing of corrections on our website (ctpub.com). If a correction is not already noted, please contact our customer service department at ctinfo@ctpub.com or P.O. Box 1456, Lafayette, CA 94549.

Trademark (™) and registered trademark (®) names are used throughout this book. Rather than use the symbols with every occurrence of a trademark or registered trademark name, we are using the names only in the editorial fashion and to the benefit of the owner, with no intention of infringement.

ISBN: 978-1-64403-621-1

Printed in China

10 9 8 7 6 5 4 3 2 1

> I wish to express my sincere thanks to Nathalie, Corinne, Sylvie, Audrey, Deborah, Alyssa, Christelle, Cindy, Johanna, Charlotte, Ambre, and Catherine who have helped me throughout this project, for both revising my writing as well as verifying the techniques used in my creations.

In this book,
YOU WILL
DISCOVER A PROGRAM
to learn the basics of crochet.

Every day for 21 days, you will either encounter new lessons or put those lessons into practice to help you master them.

The structure of this book is as follows: two consecutive days of learning and practice, then one day for a project to use what you've learned, and one day for the finishing touches.

Dedicating a little time each day to practicing is essential with any handcraft, but this is especially the case for crochet since muscle memory is very important. For this to work, you need to practice and keep practicing, even if it's only a few lines.

Once the motions become natural, then you'll be able to crochet whatever you want!

So carefully follow all the advice and tasks through the end of each day, and when you finish this book, you'll be able to have fun and create whatever projects you want!

But above all, take your time, and take it easy!

Happy crocheting!

Émilie

TABLE OF CONTENTS

Learn TO CROCHET IN 21 DAYS

Introduction	3
Glossary and abbreviations	8

LESSONS

day	1	I discover the materials	11
day	2	I start crocheting in rows	16
day	3	I learn to change colors	23

PROJECT

day	4	I crochet a phone sleeve	26
day	5	I add the final touches to my sleeve	28

LESSONS

day	6	I crochet in the front loop and the back loop	34
day	7	I learn about increases and decreases	38

PROJECT

day **8** I crochet an eco-friendly sponge: a tawashi 42

day **9** I add the final touches to my tawashi 46

LESSONS

day **10** I learn to crochet in rounds and to make
double crochets (and other stitches) 50

day **11** I learn how to increase and decrease double crochets...... 59

PROJECT

day **12** I crochet a granny square pouch 65

day **13** I add the final touches to my pouch 70

LESSONS

day **14** I learn to make a perfect circle and to use
stitch marker rings 75

day **15** I learn the tapestry or jacquard technique 78

PROJECT

day **16** I crochet a two-tone basket 82

day **17** I add the final touches to my basket 85

LESSONS

day (18) I learn to make a sphere 90

day (19) I learn how to start with an oval 98

PROJECT

day (20) I crochet an amigurumi turtle 102

day (21) I add the final touches to my turtle 106

PROJECT

bonus I crochet a shawl 110

bonus I crochet an amigurumi cat 116

ADVICE: Some helpful tips 124

GLOSSARY AND ABBREVIATIONS

ch (chain)

At the beginning of a project, make a slip knot then yarn over (take some yarn) and draw through the loop. Yarn over again and draw through the loop. Repeat as many times as needed to achieve the right number of stitches. (When chaining in the midst of a project, skip the initial slip knot.) (See Day 2)

(Color)

Indicates a color change. (See Day 3)

dec (decrease)

Insert the hook into the previous row, yarn over (take some yarn) then draw through the stitch (you now have two loops on your hook). Insert the hook into the next stitch, yarn over (take some yarn) then draw through the stitch (you now have three loops on your hook). Yarn over again then draw through all three loops. (See Day 7)

dc (double crochet)

Yarn over (take some yarn). Insert your hook into the stitch on the previous row, yarn over and draw through the work. You will now have 3 loops on your hook. Yarn over again, draw through two loops. Yarn over again and draw through the last two loops. (See Day 10)

FL (front loop) / BL (back loop)

Indicates into which loop you should crochet the row. (See Day 6)

inc (increase)

Work two single crochets into the same stitch. (See Day 7)

p (picot)

Make three chains then a slip stitch behind the first chain (in the "bump"). (See Bonus Shawl)

rnd (round)

Indicates that the work (or section) is worked in rounds. (See Day 10 and/or 14)

Glossary of Abbreviations

day 0

row

Indicates that the work (or section) is worked in rows, back and forth. (See Day 2)

sc (single crochet)

Insert your hook into the stitch in the previous row. Yarn over then draw through the stitch. Yarn over again and draw through both loops. (See Day 2)

sl st (slip stitch)

Insert your hook into the stitch in the previous row, yarn over, then draw through the work and the loop on your crochet. (See Day 10)

(Stitch count)

The stitches indicated between braces should be worked in the same stitch. (See Day 12)

... ×

Repeat the instructions between asterisks however many times are indicated by the ×. (See Day 16 or 20)

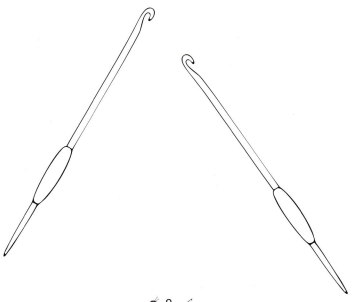

I discover THE MATERIALS

MATERIALS

Let's start with the basics: the hook and the yarn. Yarns come in different weights described with numbers (0–7) and descriptive words (lace–jumbo), which tell you how thick the yarn is. The weight of yarn is also referred to by names like Sport and Fingerling weight. If you are following a specific pattern, the pattern will tell you what weight yarn to use. The projects in this book call for 1 (super fine), 2 (fine), and 3 (light). You need to have a hook that matches the yarn with which you want to crochet.

My Advice
Choose your yarn first, then find the hook that goes with it.

You'll need a crochet hook that matches the yarn so that the yarn fits within the hook and you can form the stitches correctly. (Too small a hook and the stitch might be too tight, too large a hook and the stitch might be too loose.) All of the information you need is on the yarn label.

The yarn's weight

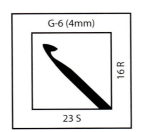

The recommended hook size

Next you will need:

– a pair of scissors (preferably one that you keep specifically for crochet and don't use for anything else),

– embroidery needles in various sizes (with rounded tips, pointed are not useful here),

– stitch marker rings (very important when making amigurumi).

I discover the materials

day 1

Marker rings used for crochet must be able to open because you will move them with each row. How to use marker rings is explained on Day 14.

My Advice

Choose marker rings that close completely. This prevents them from sliding out and losing the stitch you needed to mark.

OPTIONAL DEPENDING ON THE PROJECT

For amigurumi, you will need stuffing. That's the cotton wool you'll put inside your work (before closing it) to give it shape. Don't hesitate to really solidly stuff your work. (If you find your stitches are too loose and you're worried the stuffing will come out, first put it in some fabric before putting it into the work.)

You will also need safety eyes. These can be replaced by embroidered eyes if you prefer.

My Advice

Use safety eyes to add eyes, especially if the toy will be given to a child. How to attach these eyes is explained on Day 19.

Don't hesitate get yourself a nice little bag for all your materials. You can also invest in a row counter and tons of other crochet accessories, but this is not necessary when you're starting out.

• SOME TIPS FOR STARTING OUT RIGHT •

Here are some tips before you get started on your 21-day learning journey:

✘ Don't tighten your stitches and don't pull on the yarn after making one. It's better for your work to be too loose than too tight. Maybe this doesn't look very pretty to you with so many holes, but this is far preferable to stitches that are so tight you can't work with them.

✘ Don't take out what you've already done. Of course it's tempting to undo your work to redo it, but this will not help you understand your mistakes nor to progress. Complete Day 2, then Day 3. Are there holes, skipped stitches, places where you've pulled the yarn too tight and others where you haven't pulled enough? Not to worry, just keep going.

✘ If your crochet ever becomes too difficult to work, cut the yarn and start over. There's nothing more satisfying than seeing the progress you're making by keeping those first attempts. And this way you'll learn to understand your mistakes.

✘ Choose yarn in colors you like. The colors listed in this book are only suggestions, both for the lesson days and projects. However, I recommend darker colors (black, navy, brown, etc.).

✘ Even if certain projects list a yarn, it's best to make your first works with cotton yarn before trying out any novelty yarns. Once you're comfortable with the stitches and with the pattern, have fun with new yarns.

I discover the materials

day 1

I start CROCHETING IN ROWS

MATERIALS
- Crochet hook, size G/6 (4.00mm)
- Yarn: Weight 2 (fine)–3 (light)
- Scissors

My Advice
Don't undo what you've done, so you can see the evolution. If there are holes or dropped stitches, it's no big deal, just cut the yarn and start over. This lets you see your development and visualize the progress you're making.

THE CHAIN STITCH

Chaining is the first phase of a project worked in rows. This lesson, as well as the first row of single crochets, is one of the most complex steps in crochet, so take your time! Don't worry about your movements or how you're holding your yarn, just be careful not to make your stitches too tight.

Make a slip knot and slide it onto your hook. Don't tighten it too much; the loop should be able to slide easily on your hook.

Yarn over. This means you need to wrap your yarn around the hook. So it's easier to work with, wrap it from the back to the front over the crochet hook.

Draw the yarn you've wrapped around your hook through the loop that is already there. This creates your first stitch.

Be careful not to pull the yarn too tight around your hook!

Don't forget that your hook is there to help you, so don't hesitate to rotate it so it holds onto your yarn well during this delicate step.

Start again at Step 2: yarn over (wrap your yarn around your hook).

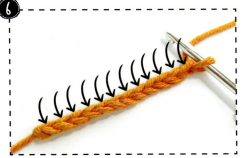

Draw the yarn that you've wrapped around your hook through the loop that is already on the hook. This creates your second stitch.

Repeat these steps until you have 12 chain stitches.

Your 12 stitches are made. You can now take a moment to count them. Each "bump" is a stitch, as indicated by the arrows.

Your chain is complete. You can repeat Steps 2–5 as many times as you like to feel comfortable with your movements, but don't hold out for perfection! Instead, I encourage you to continue: Consistency will come as you practice all the steps.

LESSON

THE SINGLE CROCHET

The single crochet is the base stitch of crochet. In every project you make, you will have single crochets. It is therefore an essential step in your learning process.

First you need to understand where the first stitch goes. The stitch at the base of your hook (indicated by the dot) can't be worked because the yarn will come out. The first stitch you can work in is the second (indicated by the arrow), then in the rest as you continue. This therefore gives you 11 stitches and not 12 (because the first stitch is never worked). Don't hesitate to count to get yourself oriented.

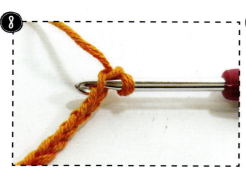

Insert your hook into the second stitch from your hook.

Yarn over (wrap your yarn around your hook).

Draw the yarn you've wrapped around your hook through the stitch into which you inserted your hook in Step 8.

You now have two loops on your hook.

Yarn over (wrap your yarn around your hook).

I start crocheting in rows

day 2

Draw the yarn you have wrapped around your hook through both loops on your hook.

You have just completed your first single crochet (indicated by the dot).

Insert your hook into the next stitch (indicated by an arrow in the previous image).

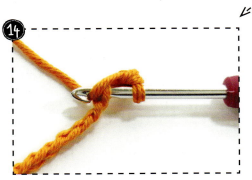

Yarn over (wrap your yarn around your hook).

My Advice

Just like with your chain, don't undo your work for every tiny mistake. This way you will see your progress with each new row, you can learn from your mistakes, and see what works and what doesn't with your movements. Nothing more satisfying than that!

Draw the yarn you've wrapped around your hook through the stitch into which you inserted your hook in Step 13.

You now have two loops on your hook.

Yarn over (wrap your yarn around your hook).

LESSON

Draw the yarn you have wrapped around your hook through both loops on your hook

You have just completed your second single crochet.

Repeat these steps for the rest of your 11 single crochets through to the end of the row (see explanation in Step 7).

This is what you will have when you finish your first row.

Before turning your work over to do the second row, you will need to make a chain stitch, just like those stitches you made when starting your work. Start by yarning over (wrap your yarn around your hook).

Draw the yarn you have wrapped around your hook through the loop already on your hook. This creates your chain stitch. Now you can turn your work over.

WHY MAKE A CHAIN STITCH AT THE END OF EACH ROW?

As explained in Step 7, you can't work in the stitch that is right at the base of your hook. Therefore you need to compensate for this loss by adding a chain stitch in order to maintain the right number of stitches in your rows.

I start crocheting in rows

day 2

This is what the back side of your work looks like. Since you've only done the one row, the stitches are not easily visible. So I recommend, to get yourself oriented, to look at the work from above.

Here is what the work looks like from above. Your stitches are more visible and they are now made up of two separate loops. Unlike the previous row where you inserted your hook through a single loop, you will now need to take up both of the stitch's loops to continue to make your single crochets.

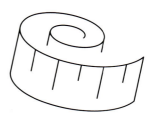

Insert your hook into the second stitch from your hook (indicated by the arrow in the previous image), making sure to pass under both loops.

Yarn over (wrap your yarn around your hook).

Draw the yarn you've wrapped around your hook through the stitch into which you inserted your hook in Step 23. You now have two loops on your hook.

Yarn over (wrap your yarn around your hook).

Draw the yarn you have wrapped around your hook through both loops on your hook.

You have just completed the first single crochet of your second row

Insert your hook into the next stitch and complete your row of 11 single crochets in total.

This is what you will have when you finish your second row with the chain at the end. Now turn the work over and continue your work in rows.

Starting from the second row, all following rows will be done exactly the same as this one.

 TODAY'S ASSIGNMENT

{ Crochet several practice rows following this exercise until you find the right movements and feel comfortable. The single crochet should become automatic since you will do it over and over again. }

See you tomorrow for our lesson on changing colors!

I learn TO CHANGE COLORS

CHANGING COLOR (IN ROWS)

Changing color at the beginning of a row is a simple process, and here you will find the different steps. Yesterday you practiced on several rows of single crochets. You will build on this work by changing colors.

MATERIALS

- Crochet hook, size G/6 (4.00mm)
- Yarn: Weight 2 (fine)–3 (light)
- Scissors

Make a row of single crochets, continuing with the color used on Day 2, and stop before you make your last stitch.

Insert your hook into the next stitch (the last of the row).

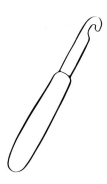

Yarn over (wrap your yarn around your hook).

Draw the yarn you have wrapped around your hook through the stitch into which you inserted the hook in Step 2.

You now have two loops on your hook

Yarn over (wrap your yarn around your hook) with the second color

It's not necessary to tie a knot, you just need to yarn over with the new yarn instead of the old one.

Draw the yarn you have wrapped around your hook through both loops on your hook.

You have just completed the last stitch of the row and joined a new yarn.

 TIP

Don't hesitate to leave long tails of yarn before joining, as this will simplify your finishing touches (Day 5).

I learn to change colors
day 3

Make your chain stitch at the end of the row with your new color, then turn the work over.

Now crochet a new row of single crochets with your new color.

There's your color change!

Cut the yarn of the first color and knot it with the second (leaving a tail of at least 2½" or 6cm).

 TODAY'S ASSIGNMENT

To practice, make several rows of single crochets with your new color, then after six rows, change color again.

Tomorrow you'll do your first crochet project!

I crochet A PHONE SLEEVE

PROJECT day 4

MATERIALS

- Crochet hook, size G/6 (4.00mm) (or whatever size is appropriate to the yarn you've chosen)
- Yarn: Weight 2 (fine)–3 (light)
  – Light pink (color 1) 27 yards (25m)
  – Dark pink (color 2) 27 yards (25m)
- Yarn needle/scissors

GLOSSARY AND ABBREVIATIONS

ch (chain)

At the beginning of a project, make a slip knot then yarn over (take some yarn) and draw through the loop. Yarn over again and draw through the loop. Repeat as many times as needed to achieve the right number of stitches. (When chaining in the midst of a project, skip the initial slip knot.) (See Day 2)

sc (single crochet)

Insert your hook into the stitch in the previous row. Yarn over then draw through the stitch. Yarn over again and draw through both loops. (See Day 2)

(Color)

Indicates a color change. (See Day 3)

row

The sleeve is worked in rows, back and forth.

This pattern creates a 4″ × 6¼″ (10 × 16cm) phone sleeve.

26

I crochet a phone sleeve

PATTERN

Row 0 = (Light pink) Start by chaining 17, turn.
Row 1–30 (30 rows) = 16 sc, 1 ch, turn.
Row 31–59 (29 rows) = (Dark pink) 16 sc, 1 ch, turn.
Row 60 = 8 sc, 15 ch, 8 sc.

Cut the yarn (leaving 4˝ or 10cm), thread it through the last loop, and pull.

STEP BY STEP

Let's take this pattern one step at a time.

Row 0: This is the foundation row: chain 17 stitches with light pink (or the color you have chosen for Color 1). (See Day 2)

Row 1–30 (30 rows): Make 16 sc (single crochets) for 30 rows (from row 1 to row 30). Be careful not to forget the chain stitch at the end of each row before turning. (See Day 2)

Row 31–59 (29 rows): Change color to dark pink (or the Color 2 you have chosen). Then crochet 29 rows of sc (single crochets) in this new color. Don't forget the chain stitch at the end of each row. (See Day 3)

Row 60: Make 8 sc (single crochets). Next ch (chain) 15, which will form the button loop to close your sleeve. Then begin again in the next stitch to do 8 sc (single crochets) again.

Finishing: Once you've completed row 60, cut your yarn, leaving 4˝ (10cm), thread it through the last loop, then pull.

Tomorrow you'll add the finishing touches!

PROJECT day 5

I add
THE FINAL TOUCHES
TO MY SLEEVE

MATERIALS

- Crochet hook, size G/6 (4.00mm)
- Yarn: Weight 2 (fine)–3 (light)
- Yarn needle/scissors
- Button

FINISHING TOUCHES

You've just made your first crocheted creation: a phone sleeve! All you have left to do are the final touches. Today, you will see how to crochet two pieces together, as well as what to do with your remaining yarn.

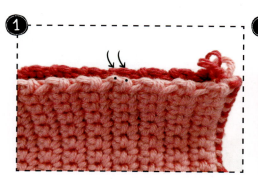

Get the sleeve in position, back against back, so the "knots" line up on both sides (they will, of course, be inverted given how the piece was made).

For example, each arrow corresponds to a point on the image.

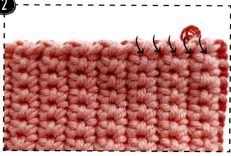

Once both sides are positioned one against the other (you can hold them in place with pins to free up your hands), you will then stitch into the "holes" between the stitches.

In the photo, these holes are indicated by arrows to guide you.

I add the final touches to my sleeve

day 5

Insert your hook through both sides.

What is represented in the photo is not the first step of these finishing touches, but something to help you see what you'll be doing.

Now let's tackle those finishing touches. Make a slip knot on your hook, then insert it through both sides of your work as shown in Step 3.

Yarn over (wrap the yarn around your hook).

Draw the yarn you have wrapped around your hook through the stitches into which you inserted your hook in Step 4.

29

PROJECT

Yarn over (wrap the yarn around your hook).

Draw the yarn you have wrapped around your hook through the two loops already on your hook

You have just made your first single crochet.

Insert your hook into the next stitch just like you did with the first stitch and make another single crochet.

You have just made your second single crochet.

Repeat these steps all along your work until the end of the row to complete the first side of your sleeve.

Don't forget the last stitch, which will go in the foundation chain and the last row.

Once this first row is complete, cut your yarn, leaving 2½" (6cm), thread it through the last loop, then pull.

Repeat Steps 4 through 11 to make the second side of your sleeve, which you will crochet in the opposite direction as the one you have just done (since we always crochet from right to left).

Once this row is complete, cut your yarn, leaving 2½" (6cm), thread it through the last loop, then pull.

I add the final touches to my sleeve

Here is the result.

Grab your yarn needle and let's deal with the remaining bits of yarn. You do not need to make a knot, but instead slide each tail between the stitches you have just made in order to hide them. Work them through a couple inches (3–4cm) to make sure they're secure.

Now cut the yarn short (having worked them through as explained in the previous step). Follow the same steps for each tail of yarn.

 TODAY'S ASSIGNMENT

Choose a button to sew onto the front of your work to close the sleeve.

Here's your first crocheted work, congratulations!

I add the final touches to my sleeve

Lesson day 6
I crochet IN THE FRONT LOOP AND THE BACK LOOP

MATERIALS
- Crochet hook, size G/6 (4.00mm)
- Yarn: Weight 2 (fine)–3 (light)
- Scissors

CROCHETING in the front loop only

Creating single crochets in only the front (or back) loop of a stitch lets you change the aesthetic of your work.

Repeat the steps from Day 2: chain 12, then crochet two rows of single crochets.

Once these rows are complete, look at the top of your work. A stitch is made up of two loops (indicated on the first 4 stitches by dots for the back loops and dashes for the front loops). Make sure to find these on your own work before beginning Step 3.

This photo serves as a reference to show you the difference when you insert through both loops of a stitch. This is not what you will be practicing today, so be aware.

I crochet in the front loop and the *back loop*

day **6**

Insert your hook through the front loop of your stitch only (indicated by a dash in Step 1) to begin your single crochet.

The steps for making a single crochet are the same as those on Day 2: yarn over, then draw through the stitch. Yarn over again, and draw through both loops on your hook.

This is what you will have.

Insert again through the front loop of the next stitch for make another single crochet and continue until you have made 11 single crochets in the row (always using the front loop only).

Here is what you will have. Since you have worked in the front loop, there will be no change on the front side of your work.

The back, however, is another story. The back loops—which you have not worked into your single crochets—are very visible. This is how using only the front loop allows you to change what your work looks like and to add texture.

CROCHETING in the back loop only

Return to Step 1 of today to work, this time, in the back loop only. Again, begin with a chain of 12 and two rows of single crochets.

You are going to insert your hook into the back loop of the stitch (indicated by a dot in Step 1) and make a single crochet.

This time, the change is much more noticeable on the front side of your work, with the stitch tucked behind the front loop.

Repeat all along the row (11 single crochets). The front loop is visible but doesn't create the same effect as that in Step 7: the single crochets are more set back.

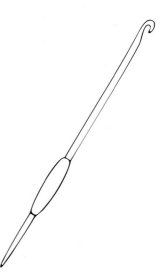

I crochet in the front loop and the back loop

day 6

As for the reverse of your work, it's again another story, as a furrow is created beneath the single crochets you have stitched.

Therefore, crocheting in the front loop only (Steps 3–7) is more discreet that crocheting in the back loop only (Steps 8–10). This visual preference will depend on how you want to add texture and which quality you want your work to have.

 TODAY'S ASSIGNMENT

Make a few rows of single crochets, alternating between front loop only and back loop only to get used to identifying the loops and to experiment with the aesthetic.

See you tomorrow for increases and decreases!

LESSON day 7

I learn about INCREASES AND DECREASES

MATERIALS
- Crochet hook, size G/6 (4.00mm)
- Yarn: Weight 2 (fine)–3 (light)
- Scissors

INCREASES AND DECREASES (single crochet)

When crocheting, increasing and decreasing single crochets lets you give shape to your creations. If you plan on making amigurumi or clothing, this step is essential.

INCREASES

Once again, follow the steps from Day 2: chain 12, then make two rows of single crochets.

Make a single crochet in the first stitch. Along this row, you will alternate between a single crochet and an increase to avoid deforming your work and getting lost.

Increase, first step: make a single crochet in the second stitch of your row.

THE SINGLE CROCHET

This stitch is made of up two loops you can discern from the top of your work, as you've learned in past days, but also two loops on the front (indicated by the arrow and two dots).

I learn about increases and decreases

Increase, second step: insert your hook through the same place you did in Step 2 (indicated by an arrow) to make a new single crochet.

So you have one foundation stitch for 2 single crochets and 4 visible loops (indicated by the dots): you have just completed your first increase.

Repeat these step for the rest of the row: alternate between one single crochet (indicated by a dot) and an increase (indicated by an arrow).

This curves your work (the choice to alternate single crochets and increases is simply to avoid making your crochet unworkable).

DECREASES

You are now going to do a row of decreases.

As with the increase, you'll start with a simple single crochet and then alternate.

Once your single crochet is complete, insert your hook into the next stitch.

39

LESSON

Yarn over (wrap your yarn around your hook).

Draw the yarn you've wrapped around your hook through the stitch into which you inserted your hook in Step 6.

You now have two loops on the hook.

Insert your hook into the next stitch.

Yarn over (wrap your yarn around your hook).

Draw the yarn you've wrapped around your hook through the stitch into which you inserted your hook in Step 9.

You now have three loops on your hook.

Yarn over (wrap your yarn around your hook).

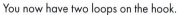

I learn about increases and decreases

Draw the yarn you've wrapped around your hook through the three loops on your hook.

You've just completed your first decrease (indicated by two dots): two loops bent to the left.

Repeat these steps for the rest of the row, alternating between one single crochet (indicated by a dot) and a decrease (indicated by an arrow).

Your work will now return to its original shape.

 TODAY'S ASSIGNMENT

Make several rows of increases and decreases to practice how they're done. Also practice identifying them by sight (don't hesitate to refer to the photos for this).

See you tomorrow for your second crochet project!

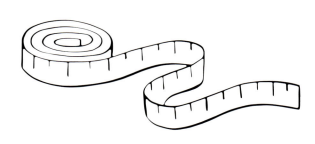

PROJECT day 8

I crochet AN ECO-FRIENDLY SPONGE : a TAWASHI

MATERIALS

- Crochet hook, size G/6 (4.00mm)
- Yarn: Weight 2 (fine)–3 (light), 100% cotton
  – Yellow 27 yards (25m)
- Yarn needle/scissors

GLOSSARY AND ABBREVIATIONS

ch (chain)

At the beginning of a project, make a slip knot then yarn over (take some yarn) and draw through the loop. Yarn over again and draw through the loop. Repeat as many times as needed to achieve the right number of stitches. (When chaining in the midst of a project, skip the initial slip knot.) (See Day 2)

sc (single crochet)

Insert your hook into the stitch in the previous row. Yarn over then draw through the stitch. Yarn over again and draw through both loops. (See Day 2)

dec (decrease)

Insert the hook into the previous row, yarn over your hook (take some yarn) then draw through the stitch (you now have two loops on your hook). Insert the hook into the next stitch, yarn over (take some yarn) then draw through the stitch (you now have three loops on your hook). Yarn over again then draw through all three loops

inc (increase)

Work two single crochets into the same stitch.

[FL] (front loop) / [BL] (back loop)

Indicates into which loop you should crochet the row.

row

The sponge is worked in rows, back and forth.

I crochet an eco-friendly sponge: a tawashi

PROJECT

PATTERN

Row 0 = Start by chaining 2, turn.
Row 1 = inc, 1 ch, turn. (2 st)
Row 2 = [BL] 2 inc, 1 ch, turn. (4 st)
Row 3 = [BL] inc, 2 sc, inc, 1 ch, turn. (6 st)
Row 4 = [BL] inc, 4 sc, inc, 1 ch, turn. (8 st)
Row 5 = [BL] inc, 6 sc, inc, 1 ch, turn. (10 st)
Row 6 = [BL] inc, 8 sc, inc, 1 ch, turn. (12 st)
Row 7 = [BL] inc, 10 sc, inc, 1 ch, turn. (14 st)
Row 8 = [BL] inc, 12 sc, inc, 1 ch, turn. (16 st)
Row 9 = [BL] inc, 14 sc, inc, 1 ch, turn. (18 st)
Row 10 = [BL] inc, 16 sc, inc, 1 ch, turn. (20 st)
Row 11 = [BL] inc, 18 sc, inc, 1 ch, turn. (22 st)
Row 12 = [BL] inc, 20 sc, inc, 1 ch, turn. (24 st)
Row 13 = [BL] inc, 22 sc, inc, 1 ch, turn. (26 st)
Row 14 = [BL] dec, 22 sc, dec, 1 ch, turn. (24 st)
Row 15 = [BL] dec, 20 sc, dec, 1 ch, turn. (22 st)
Row 16 = [BL] dec, 18 sc, dec, 1 ch, turn. (20 st)
Row 17 = [BL] dec, 16 sc, dec, 1 ch, turn. (18 st)
Row 18 = [BL] dec, 14 sc, dec, 1 ch, turn. (16 st)
Row 19 = [BL] dec, 12 sc, dec, 1 ch, turn. (14 st)
Row 20 = [BL] dec, 10 sc, dec, 1 ch, turn. (12 st)
Row 21 = [BL] dec, 8 sc, dec, 1 ch, turn. (10 st)
Row 22 = [BL] dec, 6 sc, dec, 1 ch, turn. (8 st)
Row 23 = [BL] dec, 4 sc, dec, 1 ch, turn. (6 st)
Row 24 = [BL] dec, 2 sc, dec, 1 ch, turn. (4 st)
Row 25 = [BL] 2 dec, 1 ch, turn. (2 st)
Row 26 = [BL] 1 sc, 15 ch, 1 sc.

Cut the yarn (leaving 4″ or 10cm), thread it through the last loop, and pull.

I crochet an eco-friendly sponge: *a tawashi*

day **8**

STEP BY STEP

Let's take this pattern one step at a time.

The number of st (stitches) between parentheses at the end of each row: this is useful as a guide when there are increases and decreases in a project. This lets you count your stitches in each row and get your bearings in your pattern (the ch at the end of the row doesn't count).

Row 0: This is the foundation row, so chain 2 stitches. (See Day 2)

Row 1–13: You increase single crochets in the first and last stitches of each row, from row 1 through row 13. Make sure to use the back loop only for each stitch. (See Days 6 and 7)

Row 14–25: Now you decrease single crochets in the first and last stitches of each row, from row 14 through row 25. Make sure to use the back loop only for each stitch. (See Days 6 and 7)

Row 26: Make the loop for hanging your sponge by chaining 15 between two single crochets.

Finishing: Once you've completed row 26, cut your yarn, leaving 4˝ (10cm). Thread it through your last loop then pull.

Tomorrow you'll add the finishing touches!

I add THE FINAL TOUCHES
TO MY TAWASHI

FINISHING TOUCHES

You've just made your second crocheted work: an eco-friendly sponge. All that's left is the finishing touches to tuck away the remaining yarn (see Day 5) and make a tidy crocheted border. The "sides" of a crocheted piece are actually never straight, owing to the twist of the turning stitch. It's therefore useful to add a border to give a nice finish to your work.

MATERIALS

- Crochet hook, size G/6 (4.00mm)
- Yarn: Weight 2 (fine)–3 (light)
- Yarn needle/scissors

1

Start by working the ends back in. For the bit of yarn from the foundation chain, use a needle to work the yarn through the last stitches in the row before knotting. Tuck the other end through the stitches of the preceding row.

2

Once your yarn tails are taken care of (at both the beginning and the end), you will create the border.

There are no apparent stitches to work in, so you need to alternate between bumps and spaces (indicated by a dot in the photo) to make regular single crochets.

My Advice
Watch out: don't tighten the stitches!

I add the final touches to my *tawashi*

day 9

Start on the left side of the hanger.

Make a slip knot on your hook, then insert your hook into the first bump on your sponge.

Yarn over (wrap your yarn around your hook).

Draw the yarn you've wrapped around your hook through the stitch into which you inserted your hook in Step 3.

You have two loops on your hook.

Yarn over (wrap your yarn around your hook).

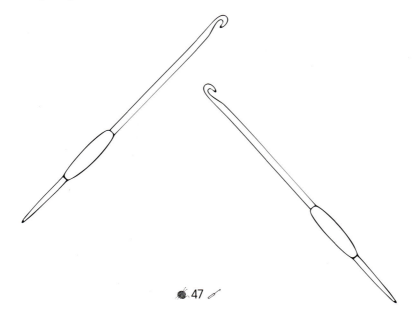

47

PROJECT

Draw the yarn you've wrapped around your hook through the two loops on your hook.

As you've surely noticed, you've just made a single crochet! Find the next space and continue with single crochets until you reach the corner.

This is what you'll have.

At each corner of the sponge (three corners), add an increase to maintain the angle.

Once you've gone around the whole sponge, cut the yarn, leaving 2½" (6cm), thread it through the last loop, then pull.

Work both ends of the yarn through a couple inches (4cm) of the stitches you have just made (see Day 5).

 TODAY'S ASSIGNMENT

{ Don't hesitate to make more in different colors or even multi-colored for practice. Plus, they're always useful. }

Here's your finished sponge. Congratulations!

48

I add the final touches to my *tawashi*

LESSON day 10

I learn

HOW TO CROCHET
IN ROUNDS AND TO MAKE DOUBLE CROCHETS

(and other stitches)

MATERIALS
- Crochet hook, size G/6 (4.00mm)
- Yarn: Weight 2 (fine)–3 (light)
- Scissors

STARTING A PROJECT WORKED IN ROUNDS USING A SERIES OF CHAINS AND A SLIP STITCH

There are two ways to start crocheting in rounds: using chain stitches or using a magic ring. The difference lies in the way the center of the round appears. With the chains, a hole will remain, but this isn't a problem when a project is made up of double crochets or if it doesn't require stuffing. That's what we'll be learning about today.

The slip stitch is a stitch that is only used when finishing a project, to shift the beginning of a work by a couple stitches, or for aesthetic reasons.

Chain 8.

Insert your hook into the first chain stitch (indicated in Step 1 by an arrow).

50

Yarn over (wrap your yarn around your hook).

Draw the yarn you've wrapped around your hook through the stitch into which you inserted your hook in Step 2 as well as through the loop on your hook.

You have just made a slip stitch to create your beginning ring.

THE DOUBLE CROCHET

The double crochet is the most-used larger stitch in crochet. It is twice as tall as a single crochet and therefore uses twice the yarn. It is principally useful in openwork projects, allowing you to form larger openings.

Repeat the steps from Day 2: chain 12 then add two rows of single crochets.

Yarn over (wrap your yarn around your hook).

My Advice

Since you will be making double crochets and other large stitches, chain 3 (instead of just one) before turning. This will let you start out with a series of chains that are the same height as your stitches.

LESSON

Insert your hook into the fourth stitch from your hook.

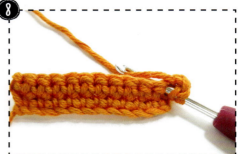

Yarn over (wrap your yarn around your hook).

Draw the yarn you've wrapped around your hook through the stitch into which you inserted your hook in Step 7.

You now have 3 loops on your hook.

Yarn over (wrap your yarn around your hook).

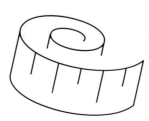

I learn to crochet *in rounds*...

day 10

Draw the yarn you've wrapped around your hook through the two left loops on your hook (so not the last one on the right).

You now have 2 loops on your hook.

Yarn over (wrap your yarn around your hook).

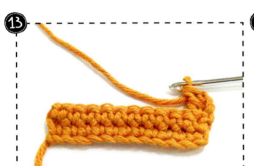

Draw the yarn you've wrapped around your hook through the two last loops.

You have just completed your first double crochet.

Start again to make another double crochet. Yarn over (wrap your yarn around your hook).

Insert your hook into the next stitch.

Yarn over (wrap your yarn around your hook).

Draw the yarn you've wrapped around your hook through the stitch into which you inserted your hook in Step 15.

You now have 3 loops on your hook.

Yarn over (wrap your yarn around your hook).

Draw the yarn you've wrapped around your hook through the two left loops on your hook (so not the last one on the right).

You now have 2 loops on your hook.

Yarn over (wrap your yarn around your hook).

Draw the yarn you've wrapped around your hook through the two last loops.

You have just completed your second double crochet.

I learn to crochet *in rounds*...

day 10

Make your 11 double crochets to finish the row.

Since the stitches are larger, they will slightly deform the work.

Here's a closer look at what you have.

WHAT DOES A DOUBLE CROCHET LOOK LIKE?

A double crochet (indicated by the big line) is much taller than a single crochet (indicated by the little line) and uses more yarn.

THE HALF DOUBLE CROCHET

The half double crochet is a medium-height stitch, between a single and double crochet.

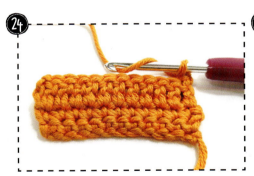

Continue from the row of double crochets. Since the half double crochet is smaller than the double crochet, only chain 2 before turning.

Yarn over (wrap your yarn around your hook) then insert your hook into the stitch of the previous row.

After inserting you hook through the work, yarn over again (wrap your yarn around your hook).

Draw the yarn you've wrapped around your hook through the stitch into which you inserted your hook in Step 24.

You now have 3 loops on your hook.

Yarn over (wrap your yarn around your hook).

Draw the yarn you've wrapped around your hook through the three loops on your hook.

You have just completed your first half double crochet.

THE TRIPLE CROCHET

The triple (or treble) crochet is even taller than the double crochet.

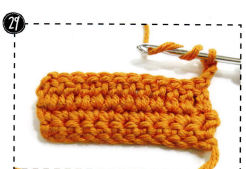

Return to Step 24 and chain 3 before turning.

Yarn over twice (wrap your yarn around your hook twice), then insert your hook into the stitch of the previous row.

After inserting you hook through the work, yarn over again (wrap your yarn around your hook).

I learn to crochet in rounds...

day 10

Draw the yarn you've wrapped around your hook through the stitch into which you inserted your hook in Step 29.

You now have 4 loops on your hook.

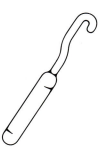

Yarn over (wrap your yarn around your hook).

Draw the yarn you've wrapped around your hook through two loops on your hook (the two on the left).

You now have 3 loops on your hook.

Yarn over (wrap your yarn around your hook).

Draw the yarn you've wrapped around your hook through two loops on your hook (the two on the left).

You now have 2 loops on your hook.

57

LESSON

Yarn over (wrap your yarn around your hook).

Draw the yarn you've wrapped around your hook through the last two loops on your hook.

You have just completed a triple crochet.

 TODAY'S ASSIGNMENT

Practice by crocheting several rows of double crochets (we'll use this stitch in our next project).

See you tomorrow for increasing and decreasing double crochets!

LESSON day 11

I learn
HOW TO INCREASE
AND DECREASE
double crochets

MATERIALS
- Crochet hook, size G/6 (4.00mm)
- Yarn: Weight 2 (fine)–3 (light)
- Scissors

INCREASING DOUBLE CROCHETS

Whether double crochets or single crochets, increasing follows the same principle: you are going to crochet two stitches into one foundation stitch.

Pick up again at Step 24 from yesterday, after your row of double crochets.

Chain 3 then turn.

Make a double crochet in the fourth stitch from your hook.

All along the row, you will alternate between a double crochet and an increase to avoid deforming the work or losing your spot.

59

Increase, first step: make a double crochet in the second stitch of your row.

Increase, second step: insert your hook into the same place as you did in Step 3 (indicated by an arrow) and make another double crochet.

So you have one foundation stitch for two double crochets. You have just completed your first increase of double crochets.

Continue like this for the rest of the row: alternate between a double crochet (indicated by a dot) and an increase (indicated by an arrow).

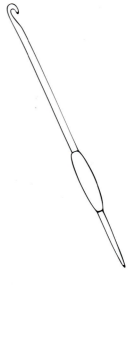

DECREASING DOUBLE CROCHETS

Decreasing double crochets is a little more complicated than decreasing single crochets, owing to the number of times you must yarn over. But with a little concentration, you'll get it done right!

You will now make a row of decreasing double crochets.

As you did with the increases, begin with one double crochet (like in Step 2) then alternate with decreases.

Yarn over (wrap your yarn around your hook).

Insert your hook into the next stitch.

Yarn over (wrap your yarn around your hook).

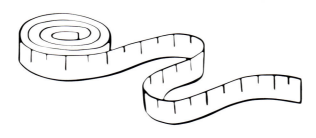

Draw the yarn you've wrapped around your hook through the stitch into which you inserted your hook in Step 8.

You now have three loops on your hook.

Yarn over (wrap your yarn around your hook).

Draw the yarn you've wrapped around your hook through the two left loops (so not the one on the right).

You now have two loops on your hook.

Yarn over (wrap your yarn around your hook).

I learn how to increase...

Insert your hook into the next stitch.

Yarn over (wrap your yarn around your hook).

Draw the yarn you've wrapped around your hook through the stitch into which you inserted your hook in Step 14.

You now have four loops on your hook.

Yarn over (wrap your yarn around your hook).

Draw the yarn you've wrapped around your hook through the two loops on the left.

You now have three loops on your hook.

Yarn over (wrap your yarn around your hook).

LESSON

Draw the yarn you've wrapped around your hook through the three last loops.

You have just completed a decrease. To find it by sight, it's a double crochet that goes over another and wraps around it at the top.

Continue like this for the rest of the row, alternating double crochets (indicated by a dot) and decreases (indicated by an arrow).

Your work will return to 11 stitches wide.

 TODAY'S ASSIGNMENT

Make several rows of increasing and decreasing double crochets to practice.

See you tomorrow for your third project.

I crochet
A GRANNY SQUARE
POUCH

MATERIALS

- Crochet hook, size G/6 (4.00mm)
- Yarn: Weight 3 (light)
  – Pink ≈ 11 yards (10m)
  – Purple ≈ 11 yards (10m)
  – Green ≈ 16½ yards (15m)
- Yarn needle/scissors

GLOSSARY AND ABBREVIATIONS

ch (chain)

At the beginning of a project, make a slip knot then yarn over (take some yarn) and draw through the loop. Yarn over again and draw through the loop. Repeat as many times as needed to achieve the right number of stitches. (When chaining in the midst of a project, skip the initial slip knot.)

sc (single crochet)

Insert your hook into the stitch in the previous row. Yarn over then draw through the stitch. Yarn over again and draw through both loops.

sl st (slip stitch)

Insert your hook into the stitch in the previous row, yarn over, then draw through the work and the loop on your crochet.

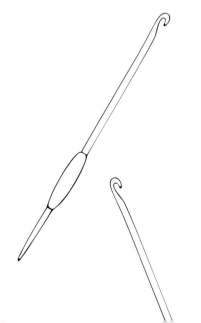

PROJECT

dc (double crochet)

Yarn over the hook (take some yarn). Insert your hook into the stitch on the previous row, yarn over and draw through the work. You will now have 3 loops on your hook. Yarn over again, draw through two loops. Yarn over again and draw through the last two loops.

inc dc (increase double crochet)

Crochet 2 dc in the same stitch.

(Color)

Indicates a color change.

{Stitch count}

The stitches indicated between braces should be worked in the same stitch.

rnd (round)

The pouch is worked in rounds.

PATTERN

rnd 0 = (green) Begin by chaining 4, then insert your hook into the first chain stitch and make 1 sl st to create a ring.

rnd 1 = inc dc, 2 ch, inc dc, 2 ch, inc dc, 2 ch, inc dc, 2 ch, 1 sl st (cut the yarn, thread it through the last loop, and pull).

rnd 2 = (pink) Starting in a corner, do the following: {2 dc, 2 ch, 2 dc, 1 ch} in each ch space of the previous round, 1 sl st. (Cut the yarn, thread it through the last loop, and pull).

rnd 3 = (purple) Starting in a corner, do the following: {2 dc, 2 ch, 2 dc}, {1 ch, 2 dc, 1 ch}, {2 dc, 2 ch, 2 dc}, {1 ch, 2 dc, 1 ch}, {2 dc, 2 ch, 2 dc}, {1 ch, 2 dc, 1 ch}, {2 dc, 2 ch, 2 dc}, {1 ch, 2 dc, 1 ch}, 1 sl st.

Cut the yarn, thread it through the last loop, and pull.
Repeat 4 times, changing the order of colors if you like.

STEP BY STEP

Let's take this pattern one step at a time.

(The colors used in these explanations are not the same as those in the pattern, but at the end of the day, there is a picture of the actual result.)

rnd 0: This is the foundation round, so chain 4 and complete the ring with a slip stitch. (See Day 10)

rnd 1: You have 4 chain stitches in your ring (indicated by dots). You will increase double crochets in each of these stitches, and don't forget the two chains between each increase. As you cannot begin a new round with a double crochet, you will need to replace the first stitch with 3 chains. You will then make one double crochet alongside these chains for the first increase. The remaining increases are just like those you learned on Day 11. The two chains between each increase will form the corners of your granny square. The slip stitch lets you complete the round. Then cut your yarn and work it in.

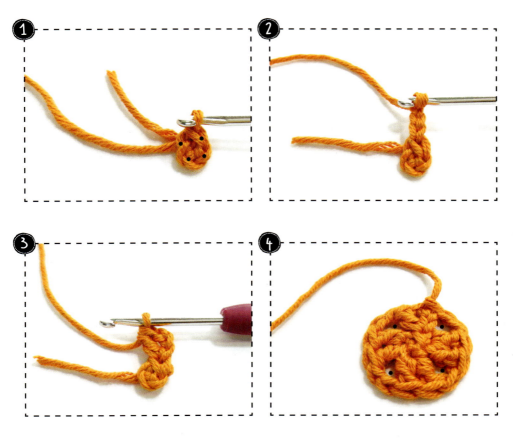

I crochet a granny square pouch — day 12

PROJECT

rnd 2: The goal is to grow your granny square, and to do this, you will need to double the amount of increases in each corner. Therefore, you will make 2 double crochets, 2 chains, 2 double crochets in each corner, and don't forget the 1 chain between each group. (Once again, replace the first double crochet with 3 chain stitches as in the previous round, and begin with a slip knot on your hook.) Don't worry about inserting your hook through the strands of the chain stitches; insert your hook into the space formed by the chains (indicated by a dot on the previous photo). The slip stitch at the end lets you complete the round. Then cut the yarn and work it in.

rnd 3: We continue growing our granny square at the corners but you now have 4 sides to work on as well. Therefore, you will do as you did in round 2: 2 double crochets, 2 chains, 2 double crochets in each corner (indicated by a dot), then 1 chain, 2 double crochets, 1 chain on each side (indicated by an arrow), before repeating: 2 double crochets, 2 chains, 2 double crochets, etc. Complete your round and make a slip stitch.

Finishing: Cut the yarn and work it in. Make 4 granny squares total and work in all the yarns. Take the time to block them. (See Some Helpful Tips, page 124).

Tomorrow, you'll tackle the finishing touches!

I crochet a granny square pouch

I add
THE FINAL TOUCHES
TO MY POUCH

FINISHING TOUCHES

You have just made four granny squares. Now you have to join them together to form a pouch. Grab a contrasting color and let's go!

MATERIALS
- Crochet hook, size G/6 (4.00mm)
- Yarn: Weight 3 (light)
- Yarn needle/Scissors
- Button

1 Gather your 4 granny squares.

2 Position them in a square to make the first seam with your hook. The seam will be vertical and also connect the two tops (indicated by the dots).

I add the final touches to my pouch

day 13

3

Insert your hook into the front loop of the right square, then the front loop of the left square. Next, make a slip knot on your hook.

4

Draw the yarn through the two front loops into which you inserted your hook in Step 3.

5

Insert your hook into the next front loop of the right square, then the left (as in Step 3), and yarn over (wrap your yarn around your hook).

6

Draw the yarn through the front loops as well as the loop on your hook (as you would for a slip stitch).
Repeat Steps 5 and 6 all along the squares.

7

This is what you will have.
Now do the same thing horizontally: slip stitches in the front loops of each square, from right to left, then the tops.

8

This is what you will have when you have completed the vertical and horizontal lines of slip stitches.
Continue to do this in the front loops all along your work to finish (not to stitch together this time, but just for the aesthetics). Also include 12 chain stitches at the top of your work to hook around your button.

71

This is what you will have.

Front view, pouch open.

Back view, pouch open.

Add a little button and your pouch is finished! Congratulations.

I add the final touches to *my* pouch

day 13

73

LESSON day 14

I learn
TO MAKE
A PERFECT CIRCLE
and to use stitch marker rings

MATERIALS
- Crochet hook, size G/6 (4.00mm)
- Yarn: Weight 2 (fine)–3 (light)
- Scissors
- Stitch marker

STARTING A SPIRAL (ROUNDS) AND STITCH MARKERS

The last lesson taught you how to work in rounds, stopping at the end of each round with a slip stitch before starting a new one. This technique is useful and invisible with double crochets, but it's rarely used for projects done with single crochets because it creates a very visible demarcation with this type of stitch. So instead the work is done in a spiral, meaning you don't end your rounds with a slip stitch. And this is where a stitch marker ring becomes indispensable—to remember where each row begins.

LESSON

Chain 6.

Insert your hook into the first chain stitch (indicated by the dot in Step 1) and make a single crochet (because you're working in a spiral, the row begins directly with a single crochet).

Thread your stitch marker through the single crochet you just made to mark the beginning of your row. So this stitch is the first.

In each stitch in your ring—and don't forget the first one, into which you just made your first single crochet (see Step 2)—you are going to increase single crochets (see Day 7) to go from 6 stitches to 12 stitches.

This is what you will have.

Once you've made your 12th single crochet, you should get to the stitch just before your stitch marker.

Remove the stitch marker, make a single crochet, then put the stitch marker into the new stitch you just made to mark the beginning of your row.

To have a perfect and flat circle, you need to increase each row by the number of stitches in your beginning chain (in this case, 6), so next go from 12 stitches to 18.

To do this, you will increase in every other stitch, which will look like this in the pattern:

***1 sc, inc* ×6**

... × : Repeat the instructions between asterisks however many times are indicated by the ×.

I learn to make a perfect circle...

You now have 18 stitches. Once you've made your 18th single crochet, you should get to the stitch just before your stitch marker.

Remove the stitch marker, make a single crochet, then put the stitch marker into the new stitch you just made to mark the beginning of your row.

Now you need to go from 18 to 24 stitches. You will therefore add an increase every third stitch:

1 sc, inc, *2 sc, inc* ×5, 1 sc

Or, more simply, you can do:

***2 sc, inc* ×6**

but it's better to offset the placement of the increase from one row to the next so you don't wind up with a hexagon instead of a circle.

 TODAY'S ASSIGNMENT

You can continue practicing by increasing each row by 6 stitches like so:

3 sc, inc ×6 (30 st)
2 sc, inc, *4 sc, inc* ×5, 2 sc (36 st)
5 sc, inc ×6 (42 st)
3 sc, inc, *6 sc, inc* ×5, 3 sc (48 st)...

See you tomorrow for our lesson in tapestry crochet!

Lesson day 15

I learn THE TAPESTRY OR JACQUARD TECHNIQUE

TAPESTRY CROCHET

Tapestry crochet, also known as jacquard, lets you create patterns by changing colors several times within the same row. To do this, you don't cut the yarn, but rather make it run behind the work by wrapping it with the working yarn so you can pick it back up in a few stitches. Be careful: your thread tension is very important. You mustn't pull too tight nor leave it too loose.

MATERIALS

- Crochet hook, size G/6 (4.00mm)
- Yarn: Weight 2 (fine)–3 (light)
- Scissors
- Stitch marker

Start at the beginning of a round and make your first single crochet.

Start your second single crochet, but don't complete the last step.

My Advice

Don't forget to place the marker ring in your single crochet.

I learn the tapestry or jacquard technique

When you're at the point of drawing the yarn through the two loops to create the single crochet, take up the second color (as you learned on Day 3). Here, the second color is green.

Draw the new yarn through the two loops on your hook. This allows you to begin the next stitch with the new color and to avoid any gap.

You are now going to make a single crochet with the second color (green). The first yarn (orange) should run along the reverse of your work to be held in place by your next stitches.

You have several options for how to position it. (See Steps 10 and 11)

Yarn over, then draw the yarn through the stitch into which you inserted your hook in the previous step.

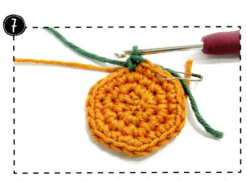

Complete you first single crochet in the new color, then make a second.

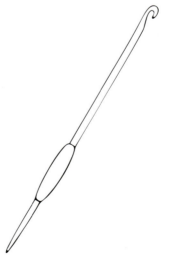

LESSON

When making the third, stop before the last step to return to the orange yarn you've kept with you.

Here is what you will have. You can now start your next three single crochets in orange (don't forget to run the green yarn behind).

Here's the first method of maintaining your non-working yarn: you leave it behind your work, sandwiching it between the work and the yarn you're working with.

If you're worried about messing up which thread to use having both behind the work, you can run your non-working thread over the stitches.

Once your three orange single crochets are complete, remember to change yarns in the last step of your third stitch and continue these steps for the whole round, alternating every three stitches.

I learn the tapestry or jacquard technique

Here's what you'll have on the reverse of your work when running the yarn behind.

You can also see that when working in rounds, stitches on the front and back of your work are not identical (unlike when working in rows).

After you've finished the row, this is what you will have. As there were no increases this time, the work begins to curve.

 TODAY'S ASSIGNMENT

Continue with your tapestry crochet for several rows. The work will rise to form the bottom of a cylinder. Don't forget to use your stitch marker ring, and have fun shifting your colors if you'd like, now is the time to try it out. This will help with your thread tension as well.

See you tomorrow for your fourth project.

PROJECT day 16

I crochet A TWO-TONE BASKET

GLOSSARY AND ABBREVIATIONS

ch (chain)

At the beginning of a project, make a slip knot then yarn over (take some yarn) and draw through the loop. Yarn over again and draw through the loop. Repeat as many times as needed to achieve the right number of stitches.

sc (single crochet)

Insert your hook into the stitch in the previous row. Yarn over then draw through the stitch. Yarn over again and draw through both loops.

sl st (slip stitch)

Insert your hook into the stitch in the previous row, yarn over, then draw through the work and the loop on your crochet.

inc (increase)

Work two single crochets into the same stitch.

(Color)

Indicates a color change.

MATERIALS

- Crochet hook, size G/6 (4.00mm)
- Yarn: Weight 2 (fine)–3 (light), chenille
  – Burgundy ≈ 44 yards (40m)
  – Turquoise ≈ 16½ yards (15m)
- Yarn needle/scissors
- Stitch marker

I crochet a two-tone basket

... ×

Repeat the instructions between asterisks however many times are indicated by the ×.

FL (front loop) / BL (back loop)

Indicates into which loop you should crochet the row.

rnd (round)

The basket is worked in rounds.

PATTERN

rnd 0 = (burgundy) Start by chaining 6 then insert your hook through the first chain stitch to form a ring.

rnd 1 = 6 inc (12 st)

rnd 2 = *1 sc, inc* ×6 (18 st)

rnd 3 = 1 sc, inc, *2 sc, inc* ×5, 1 sc (24 st)

rnd 4 = *3 sc, inc* ×6 (30 st)

rnd 5 = 2 sc, inc, *4 sc, inc* ×5, 2 sc (36 st)

rnd 6 = *5 sc, inc* ×6 (42 st)

rnd 7 = 3 sc, inc, *6 sc, inc* ×5, 3 sc (48 st)

rnd 8 = *7 sc, inc* ×6 (54 st)

rnd 9 = 4 sc, inc, *8 sc, inc* ×5, 4 sc (60 st)

rnd 10 = *9 sc, inc* ×6 (66 st)

rnd 11 = 5 sc, inc, *10 sc, inc* ×5, 5 sc (72 st)

rnd 12 = [BL] 72 sc (72 st)

rnd 13 = 72 sc (72 st)

rnd 14 and 15: shift your stitch marker one stitch back at the end of each round.

rnd 14 = *(turquoise) 1 sc, (burgundy) 5 sc* ×11, *(turquoise) 1 sc, (burgundy) 4 sc* (71 st)

rnd 15 = *(turquoise) 3 sc, (burgundy) 3 sc* ×11, *(turquoise) 3 sc, (burgundy) 2 sc* (71 st)

rnd 16 = *(turquoise) 5 sc, (burgundy) 1 sc* ×12 (72 st)

rnd 17–19 (3 rnds) = (turquoise) 72 sc (72 st)

Make 1 sl st and cut the yarn.

PROJECT

STEP BY STEP

Let's take this pattern one step at a time.

rnd 0: This is the foundation round so chain 5 and turn it into a ring with a single crochet (See Day 14). Don't forget to place your stitch marker: this single crochet is the first of round 1.

rnd 1–11: These are the increasing rounds for the base of the basket. (see Day 14)

rnd 12: Use the back loop only for this round to create a nice border between the base and sides of the basket.

rnd 14–15: You will start your tapestry technique in round 14. As you're working in a spiral (without closing each round), you will need to shift your stitch marker one stitch backward at the end of these rounds. Remember to properly position your non-working yarn. (See Day 15)

rnd 16: Last round of tapestry, don't move your stitch marker anymore.

rnd 17–19: These are three normal rounds of turquoise.

Finishing: Make a slip stitch and cut the thread (leaving 4˝ or 10cm).

Tomorrow we tackle the finishing touches!

PROJECT day 17

I add THE FINAL TOUCHES TO MY BASKET

MATERIALS

- Crochet hook, size G/6 (4.00mm)
- Yarn: Weight 2 (fine)–3 (light), chenille
  – Burgundy ≈ 11 yards (10m)
- Yarn needle/scissors
- Stitch marker

FINISHING TOUCHES

You have just made your basket. We're going to look at how to close your round invisibly, since you've worked in a spiral. Then you will add a shell finish.

You already made a slip stitch (indicated by a dot) to finish your round. Now draw your yarn through your stitch and grab your needle. Thread the yarn from the front to the back in the second stitch from your slip stitch (indicated by an arrow).

Pull your yarn until it's the same size at the stitches around it.

PROJECT

Insert your needle into the slip stitch that you made to finish your work yesterday (indicated by a dot).

This creates a stitch that hides your closing. Then work the yarn back in as you've learned in previous finishing touches: by threading it through the other stitches.

Now you're going to make a decorative border. Make a slip knot on your hook then make a slip stitch in a single crochet.

Don't work in the next stitch (indicated by a dot) and make 4 double crochets in the one after that (indicated by an arrow).

Don't work in the next stitch (indicated by a dot) and make a slip stitch in the one after that (indicated by an arrow).

You have just made your first shell.

Repeat Steps 6 and 7 all around the work.

Finish with 4 double crochets. Cut the yarn and pull it through the loop on your hook.

86

I add the final touches to my basket

With a needle, thread the yarn into the first slip stitch of your round.

Then thread the yarn through the loop of your last double crochet.

Now you can make a knot with your beginning yarn and your finishing yarn before hiding them like the others, along the stitches.

Here is your finished basket, congratulations!

I add the final touches to *my basket*

I learn TO MAKE A SPHERE

MATERIALS
- Crochet hook, size G/6 (4.00mm)
- Yarn: Weight 2 (fine)–3 (light)
- Stuffing
- Scissors
- Stitch marker

THE MAGIC RING AND MAKING A SPHERE

As explained on Day 10, there are two ways to start a project worked in rounds: starting with a chain or with a magic ring. It's the latter that we'll work on today. It will let you make amigurumi which require a solid circle to avoid any stuffing coming out.

Wrap the yarn around your fingers from left to right (the end of you yarn will therefore be on the right). Hold the yarn between your fingers to create the right tension.

Here's a second view of the yarn's placement.

I learn to make a sphere

day 18

Slide the hook under the first strand to get the other (the one on the left).

Draw the yarn under the first strand from Step 3 to create a loop on your hook.

Yarn over (wrap the yarn around your hook).

Draw the yarn you've wrapped around your hook through the loop on your hook.

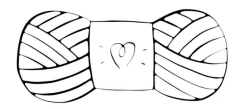

91

You can now very gently remove the ring from your fingers to let yourself work around it.

My Advice
It's not easy to work with so little material in your hands, so proceed cautiously and try not to pull on the thread so you don't close the ring.

Insert your hook through the ring.

Yarn over (wrap the yarn around your hook).

I learn to make a sphere

day 18

Draw the yarn you've wrapped around your hook through the ring.

Yarn over (wrap the yarn around your hook).

Draw the yarn you've wrapped around your hook through the two loops on your hook.

This is the first single crochet on your ring, make 5 more (6 in total) by repeating Steps 8 through 12.

Here are the 6 single crochets you will have.

I'd recommend removing your hook for this last step, so enlarge your loop so you don't lose it (indicated by a dot).

Then pull on the yarn at the end (indicated by an arrow).

Here's what you will have after pulling on the yarn.

My Advice
The ring can reopen. To avoid this happening, make a knot right now on the back side of your work by pulling tight on the yarn. This way, it won't move anymore.

 • ANOTHER METHOD

So that the ring stayed totally secure, there is another method (with the yarn wrapped twice around your fingers in Step 1), but it's more complicated, so I recommend only considering this other method once you've mastered the first technique.

Make a single crochet in the first stitch of your ring and place a stitch marker in it to note your spot. Now you'll continue as you learned on Day 14.
Make: **6 inc**.

Once you've reached 12 stitches, make a second round of increases like this:

1 sc, inc ×6

I learn to make a sphere

day 18

You have 18 stitches.

To make a perfect sphere, you need to have as many rounds without increases as you have with increases. You're therefore going to have 2 rounds of 18 single crochets so that your work curves.

Here's what you'll have at the end of two rounds of 18 single crochets.

Here's the view from above.

You can see that the beginning yarn in not worked back in. There's no reason to since you'll be closing the work to make a sphere.

Now make a round of decreases like this:

1 sc, dec ×6.

Important

When you crochet in rounds, there is a front and back to your work. You need to see the stitches as they are in the photo (with only vertical loops) to make sure you're in the right orientation.

LESSON

You're now back to 12 stitches.

Make another round of decreases like this:
6 dec.

You're back to 6 stitches. Pack the sphere with stuffing.

My Advice
The stuffing needs to be packed in tightly to make sure it holds its shape over time, so even if it seems too hard at first, this will allow the shape to remain.

To close the last 6 stitches correctly, grab your needle.

You are going to insert the needle into each front loop of the last 6 stitches (indicated by a dot).

96

I learn to make a sphere

day 18

Once the yarn is threaded through these 6 stitches, pull tight on the yarn.

Once your sphere is complete, you can thread the yarn under the stitches to hold it in place.

Here's the final result.

 TODAY'S ASSIGNMENT

You can make a few spheres for practice, because this will be helpful for your upcoming project.

See you tomorrow for your lesson in ovals!

97

LESSON day 19

I learn
HOW TO START
WITH AN OVAL

MATERIALS
- Crochet hook, size G/6 (4.00mm)
- Yarn: Weight 2 (fine)–3 (light)
- Scissors
- Stuffing
- Safety eyes
- Stitch marker

STARTING WITH AN OVAL
Certain projects have an oval foundation instead of a circle. These you must start with a chain.

Chain 6.

Insert your hook into the second stitch from your hook and make a single crochet. You are now working on your first row, just as you learned on Day 2.

Place your stitch marker in this first single crochet to keep track of it.

I learn how to start with *an oval*

day 19

Make 3 single crochets, giving you 4 in total (indicated by the dots). So only the last stitch remains to be worked (indicated by the arrow).

Make a triple increase, meaning 3 single crochets in the last stitch of the row (indicated by an arrow in Step 3).

Don't turn your work over, but continue onto the other side of the beginning chain to make single crochets that mirror your earlier ones.

Make 3 single crochets (indicated by the dots).

One stitch is left before your stitch marker.

In this last stitch, make an increase, meaning two single crochets in the same stitch.

You have now finished your round.

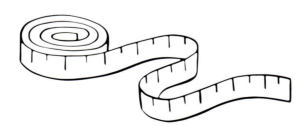

99

Make a single crochet in the first stitch of the previous turn (the one with the stitch marker).

You now have 12 stitches. You have started your first oval.

PLACING SAFETY EYES

Safety eyes are recommended for projects because, as the name would imply, they can be completely and safely secured.

A safety eye is made up of the eye (in whichever color you choose) and the washer that allows it to be secured.

In the pattern, you will find an instruction as to the row where you will add the eyes as well as the number of stitches between the eyes.

If it tells you to put the eyes between rounds 10 and 11, it's best to go as far as round 14 before placing the eyes so you have enough material to do so.

Push the eyes into your work.

Please note
It's always best practice to embroider eyes onto any amigurumi intended for a child.

I learn how to start with *an oval*

day 19

Once they're in position, turn the piece over to work on the reverse side.

Slide the washers onto the stems of the eyes and press them until the work is tightly sandwiched between the eye and the washer.

You have secured your eyes, and they won't move anymore.

Optional: If you have pliers and you need to cut the stem because they're altering the shape of your work, you can cut off the very end of the stem (no more than 1/16″ or a couple millimeters!) then heat and flatten them. This way they will be wider and stay in place

 TODAY'S ASSIGNMENT

Get your yarn, stuffing, eyes, and hook ready for your amigurumi.

See you tomorrow to make your first amigurumi!

101

I crochet AN AMIGURUMI TURTLE

PROJECT day 20

MATERIALS

- Crochet hook, size D/3 (3.25mm)
- Yarn: Weight 1 (super fine)–2 (fine)
  – Blue ≈ 16½ yards (15m)
  – Gray ≈ 11 yards (10m)
- Stuffing
- Yarn needle/scissors
- 2 safety eyes ¼" (6mm) *(or black yarn for stitching)*

GLOSSARY AND ABBREVIATIONS

Magic ring
See Day 18.

sc (single crochet)
Insert your hook into the stitch in the previous row. Yarn over then draw through the stitch. Yarn over again and draw through both loops.

sl st (slip stitch)
Insert your hook into the stitch in the previous row, yarn over, then draw through the work and the loop on your crochet.

dec (decrease)
Insert the hook into the previous row, yarn over your hook (take some yarn) then draw through the stitch (you now have two loops on your hook). Insert the hook into the next stitch, yarn over (take some yarn) then draw through the stitch (you now have three loops on your hook). Yarn over again then draw through all three loops.

inc (increase)
Work two sc into the same stitch.

... x
Repeat the instructions between asterisks however many times are indicated by the x.

rnd (round)
The amigurumi is worked in a spiral.

I crochet an amigurumi turtle

PATTERN

Shell—Bottom Blue

rnd 0 = Start with a magic ring.
rnd 1 = 6 sc in the ring (6 st)
rnd 2 = 6 inc (12 st)
rnd 3 = *1 sc, inc* ×6 (18 st)
rnd 4 = 1 sc, inc, *2 sc, inc* ×5, 1 sc (24 st)
rnd 5 = *3 sc, inc* ×6 (30 st)
rnd 6 = 2 sc, inc, *4 sc, inc* ×5, 2 sc (36 m)

Finish with a sl st. Cut and work the yarn back in.

Shell—Top Blue

rnd 0 = Start with a magic ring.
rnd 1 = 6 sc in the ring (6 st)
rnd 2 = 6 inc (12 st)
rnd 3 = *1 sc, inc* ×6 (18 st)
rnd 4 = 1 sc, inc, *2 sc, inc* ×5, 1 sc (24 st)
rnd 5 = *3 sc, inc* ×6 (30 st)
rnd 6 = 30 sc
rnd 7 = 2 sc, inc, *4 sc, inc* ×5, 2 sc (36 st)
rnd 8–10 (3 rnds) = 36 sc

Leave your yarn on hold to use for final touches tomorrow.

Feet Gray

rnd 0 = Start with a magic ring.
rnd 1 = 6 sc in the ring (6 st)
rnd 2 = *1 sc, inc* ×3 (9 st)
rnd 3 = 9 sc
rnd 4 = *1 sc, dec* ×3 (6 st)

Finish with a sl st and stuff. Cut and work the yarn back in (leaving 4″ or 10cm for sewing).
Make 4 feet total.

PROJECT

Tail Gray

rnd 0 = Start with a magic ring.
rnd 1 = 3 sc in the ring (3 st)
rnd 2 = 3 inc (6 st)

Finish with a sl st. Cut and work the yarn back in (leaving 4" or 10cm for sewing).

Head Gray

rnd 0 = Start with a magic ring.
rnd 1 = 6 sc in the ring (6 st)
rnd 2 = 6 inc (12 st)
rnd 3 = *1 sc, inc* ×6 (18 st)
rnd 4 = 1 sc, inc, *2 sc, inc* ×5, 1 sc (24 st)
rnd 5–7 = 24 sc

➤ Place the safety eyes between rows 6 and 7 with 6 stitches between them.

rnd 8 = 1 sc, dec, *2 sc, dec* ×5, 1 sc (18 st)
rnd 9 = *1 sc, dec* ×6 (12 st)
rnd 10 = 12 sc

Finish with a sl st and stuff. Cut and work the yarn back in.

STEP BY STEP

Let's take this pattern one step at a time.

You're going to make each part of the turtle today using the pattern and experience. You will assemble the turtle tomorrow.

Apart from the top of the shell, you will finish each part with a sl st (keeping a length of yarn for sewing when indicated) as you learned when finishing the basket. (See Day 17)

Head : Don't forget to add the safety eyes before stuffing. (See Day 19)

See you tomorrow for the turtle's finishing touches!

I crochet an amigurumi turtle

I add
THE FINAL TOUCHES
TO MY TURTLE

MATERIALS

- Crochet hook, size D/3 (3.25mm)
- Yarn: Weight 1 (super fine)–2 (fine) – Blue ≈ 1 foot (30cm)
- Stuffing
- Yarn needle/scissors
- Ball head pins (for positioning the components)

FINISHING TOUCHES

You have the individual pieces of a turtle, and that's a good start. Now, on to the sewing!

Sewing the Shell, top and bottom

Begin by taking the top of the shell with its yarn on hold to crochet it together with the bottom of the shell (you are crocheting together two pieces as you did during your first project), adding an additional round (the 11th) like this: *5 sc, **inc*** × 6 (42 st).

I add the final touches to *my turtle*

> **Please note**
> You need to take both loops from the <u>top</u> of the shell and the front loop from the <u>bottom</u> of the shell.

Stop 6 stitches before the end of the round to only work in one piece (namely, the top of the shell) as this will create the opening for the head (see photo). Once the round is finished, make a slip stitch then cut the yarn and work it back in. Stuff well, the oval shape will form on its own.

Sewing Feet and Tail

Once you've sewn the shell, use ball head pins to properly position the four feet and the tail. Place the feet so the turtle will be stable, with the tail between the back legs.

PROJECT

Sewing Head and Shell

All that's left is the head. Take your blue yarn and make a knot in a stitch on the head. You have 12 stitches on the head and 12 on the body. Properly position the head with pins to line up the stitches, and begin sewing between the stitches, going from right to left, tightening the yarn so there are no holes.

You may have to start over a few times to get the technique right. This is perfectly normal, so don't get down. Once the head is sewn on, work the yarn back into your work.

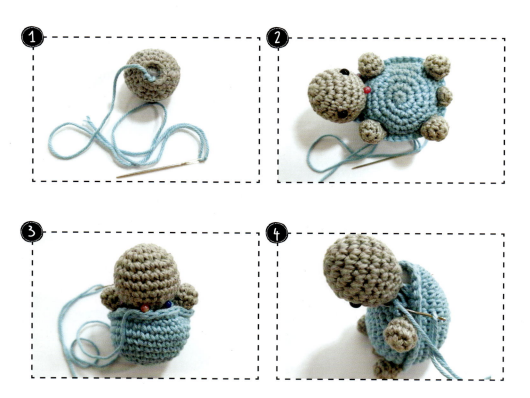

And here's your first amigurumi. Bravo!

I add the final touches to *my* turtle

day 21

109

I crochet
A SHAWL

MATERIALS

- Crochet hook, size G/6 (4.00mm)
- Yarn: Weight 3 (light)
  – Multicolored ≈ 600 yards (550m)
- Yarn needle/scissors

GLOSSARY AND ABBREVIATIONS

ch (chain)

At the beginning of a project, make a slip knot then yarn over (take some yarn) and draw through the loop. Yarn over again and draw through the loop. Repeat as many times as needed to achieve the right number of stitches. (When chaining in the midst of a project, skip the initial slip knot.)

sc (single crochet)

Insert your hook into the stitch in the previous row. Yarn over then draw through the stitch. Yarn over again and draw through both loops.

sl st (slip stitch)

Insert your hook into the stitch in the previous row, yarn over, then draw through the work and the loop on your crochet.

p (picot)

Make three chains then a slip stitch behind the first chain (in the "bump").

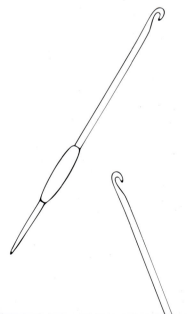

dc (double crochet)

Yarn over the hook (take some yarn). Insert your hook into the stitch on the previous row, yarn over and draw through the work. You will now have 3 loops on your hook. Yarn over again, draw through two loops. Yarn over again and draw through the last two loops.

FL (front loop) / BL (back loop)

Indicates into which loop you should crochet the row.

{Stitch count}

The stitches indicated between braces should be worked in the same stitch.

row

The shawl is worked in rows, back and forth.

PROJECT

PATTERN

Important
- Double crochets are made around the chains of the preceding row (don't bother trying to work in whichever loop, just surround it). They are typed in bold letters to help you spot them.
- For each row of single crochets, the chains are done in the same place as the chains in the previous row, you therefore only work in the back loops of the chains. This row gives texture to you work.
- The first six rows of the shawl correspond to those you will repeat throughout the shawl. So you'll see that your work will go very quickly once you've mastered the repetition.
- The stitches between {...} correspond to the point of your triangular shawl.
- Unusually, the chains are made at the beginning of the row.

row 0 = Begin by chaining 6 then insert your hook into the first chain stitch and make 1 sl st to form the ring.
row 1 = In the ring: 4 ch, **3 dc**, 2 ch, **3 dc**, 1 ch, **1 dc**, turn.
row 2 = 4 ch, **3 dc**, 1 ch, {**3 dc**, 2 ch, **3 dc** = point}, 1 ch, **3 dc**, 1 ch, **1 dc**, turn.
row 3 = [BL] 2 ch, 3 sc, 1 ch, 3 sc, 2 ch, 3 sc, 1 ch, 3 sc, 1 ch, 1 sc, turn.
row 4 = 4 ch, ***3 dc**, 1 ch* × 2, {**3 dc**, 2 ch, **3 dc** = point}, *1 ch, **3 dc*** × 2, 1 ch, **1 dc**, turn.
row 5 = 4 ch, ***3 dc**, 1 ch* × 3, {**3 dc**, 2 ch, **3 dc** = point}, *1 ch, **3 dc*** × 3, 1 ch, **1 dc**, turn.
row 6 = [FL] 2 ch, *3 sc, 1 ch* × 3, 3 sc, 2 ch, 3 sc, *1 ch, 3 sc* × 3, 1 ch, 1 sc, turn.

These are the first six rows for beginning your shawl. The next 6 will be those you'll repeat until you reach the desired size. So that you can refer back to them, the number of repetitions will now longer be indicated like *3 dc, 1 ch* × 3, since this will increase with each row. It will therefore be replaced with *3 dc, 1 ch* × until the point or *3 dc, 1 ch* × until the end of the row, to suit all rows.

rows 7–8 (2 rows) = **4 ch**, *3 dc, **1 ch*** × until the point, {3 dc, **2 ch**, 3 dc = point}, *****1 ch**, 3 dc*** × juntil the end of the row, **1 ch**, 1 dc, turn.

row 9 = [BL] **2 ch**, *3 sc, **1 ch*** × until 3 st before the point, 3 sc, **2 ch**, 3 sc, *****1 ch**, 3 ms*** × until the end of the row, **1 ch**, 1 sc, turn

rows 10–11 (2 rows) = **4 ch**, *3 dc, **1 ch*** × until the point, {3 dc, **2 ch**, 3 dc = point}, *****1 ch**, 3 dc*** × until the end of the row, **1 ch**, 1 dc, turn.

row 12 = [FL] **2 ch**, *3 sc, **1 ch*** × until 3 st before the point, 3 sc, **2 ch**, 3 sc, *****1 ch**, 3 sc*** × until the end of the row, **1 ch**, 1 sc, turn.

Repeat these 6 rows (7–12) another 7 times (through row 54) then:

rows 55–56 (2 rows) = **4 ch**, *3 dc, **1 ch*** × until the point, {3 dc, **2 ch**, 3 dc = point}, *****1 ch**, 3 dc*** × until the end of the row, **1 ch**, 1 dc, turn.

row 57 = [BL] **2 ch**, *3 sc, **1 ch*** × until 3 st before the point, 3 sc, **2 ch**, 3 sc, *****1 ch**, 3 sc*** × until the end of the row, **1 ch**, 1 sc, turn.

Now you will create the border by making arches over the single crochets for a first row, then working in them for the second.

row 58 = *6 ch, skip 3 stitches, 1 sl st in the ch of the previous row* × until the end of the row, turn.

row 59 = 4 sc in the first arch, *{4 dc, 3 ch, 4 dc in the next arch}, 1 sl st in the following one* × until 1 arch before the point, 6 dc, picot, 6 dc, *1 sl st in the next arch, {4 dc, 3 ch, 4 dc in the following one}* × until 1 arch before the end of the row, 4 sc in the last arch.

**Finish with a slip stitch, cut the thread and work it back in.
Work the other threads in and then take the time to block your shawl (See Some Helpful Tips, page 124) to achieve its fullest potential.**

I crochet AN AMIGURUMI CAT

MATERIALS

- Crochet hook, size D/3 (3.25mm)
- Yarn: Weight 1 (super fine)–2 (fine)
  - White ≈ 16½ yards (15m)
  - Gray ≈ 71 yards (65m)
  - Blue ≈ 5½ yards (5m)
- Stuffing
- Yarn needle/scissors
- 2 safety eyes ¼" (6mm) *(or black yarn for stitching)*

GLOSSARY AND ABBREVIATIONS

Magic ring
See Day 18.

sc (single crochet)
Insert your hook into the stitch in the previous row. Yarn over then draw through the stitch. Yarn over again and draw through both loops.

sl st (slip stitch)
Insert your hook into the stitch in the previous row, yarn over, then draw through the work and the loop on your crochet.

dec (decrease)
Insert the hook into the previous row, yarn over your hook (take some yarn) then draw through the stitch (you now have two loops on your hook). Insert the hook into the next stitch, yarn over (take some yarn) then draw through the stitch (you now have three loops on your hook). Yarn over again then draw through all three loops.

inc (increase)
Work two sc into the same stitch.

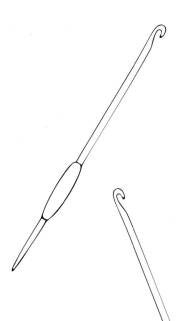

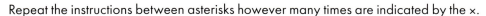

... ×
Repeat the instructions between asterisks however many times are indicated by the ×.

rnd (round)
The amigurumi is worked in a spiral.

row
This section of the amigurumi is worked in rows, back and forth.

p (picot)
Make three chains then a slip stitch behind the first chain (in the "bump").

 PATTERN

Head Gray

rnd 0 = Start with a magic ring.
rnd 1 = 6 sc in the ring (6 st)
rnd 2 = 6 inc (12 st)
rnd 3 = *1 sc, inc* ×6 (18 st)
rnd 4 = 1 sc, inc, *2 sc, inc* ×5, 1 sc (24 st)
rnd 5 = *3 sc, inc* ×6 (30 st)
rnd. 6 = 2 sc, inc, *4 sc, inc* ×5, 2 sc (36 st)
rnd 7 = *5 sc, inc* ×6 (42 st)
rnd 8-12 (5 rnds) = 42 sc ➤ Place the safety eyes between rows 9 and 10 with 7 stitches between them.
rnd 13 = *5 sc, dec* ×6 (36 st)
rnd. 14 = 2 sc, dec, *4 sc, dec* ×5, 2 sc (30 st) ➤ Start stuffing.
rnd 15 = *3 sc, dec* ×6 (24 st)

Firmly stuff, finish with a slip stitch, and cut the yarn. Don't forget to leave enough yarn for sewing (see remaining steps). Use the black yarn for stitching the nose and whiskers (see photos).

PROJECT

Ears Gray and white

You will be working back and forth, so make sure to begin your rows in the second stitch from your hook and make the chain stitch at the end of each row (as indicated).

row 0 = (gray or white) Begin by chaining 6.
row 1 = 5 sc, 1 ch, and turn (5 st)
row 2 = dec, 3 sc, 1 ch, and turn (4 st)
row 3 = dec, 2 sc, 1 ch, and turn (3 st)
row 4 = dec, 1 sc, 1 ch, and turn (2 st)
row 5 = dec (1 st)

Cut the yarn and work it in.
Follow this pattern to make 2 gray ears and 2 white ears.

Take one gray ear and one white ear and put them together (white on the back, gray in front) then assemble them with a round of sc using gray yarn, inserting your hook through both stitches (gray and white). No need to stitch the base of the ear, the two sides are enough.

Cut the yarn. Don't forget to leave enough yarn for sewing (see remaining steps).
Assemble the second ear in the same way.

My Advice
To make a pointier ear, you can add an increase in the sc at the top.

I crochet an amigurumi cat

Body Gray

rnd 0 = Begin with a magic ring.
rnd 1 = 6 sc in the ring (6 st)
rnd 2 = 6 inc (12 st)
rnd 3 = *1 sc, inc* ×6 (18 st)
rnd 4 = 1 sc, inc, *2 sc, inc* ×5, 1 sc (24 st)
rnd 5 = *3 sc, inc* ×6 (30 st)
rnd 6 = 2 sc, inc, *4 sc, inc* ×5, 2 sc (36 st)
rnd 7 = *5 sc, inc* ×6 (42 st)
rnd 8 = 3 sc, inc, *6 sc, inc* ×5, 3 sc (48 st)
rnd 9–13 (5 rnds) = 48 sc
rnd 14 = 3 sc, dec, *6 sc, dec* ×5, 3 sc (42 st)
rnd 15–16 (2 rnds) = 42 sc
rnd 17 = *5 sc, dec* ×6 (36 st)
rnd 18–20 (3 rnds) = 36 sc ▷ Start stuffing.
rnd 21 = 2 sc, dec, *4 sc, dec* ×5, 2 sc (30 st)
rnd 22–24 (3 rnds) = 30 sc
rnd 25 = *3 sc, dec* ×6 (24 st)
rnd 26–27 (2 rnds) = 24 sc

Finish with a sl st. Cut the yarn and work it in. Firmly stuff.

Arms Gray and white

rnd 0 = (white) Start with a magic ring.
rnd 1 = 6 sc in the ring (6 st)
rnd 2 = *1 sc, inc* ×3 (9 st)
rnd 3–4 (2 rnds) = 9 sc
rnd 5–9 (5 rnds) = (gray) 9 sc

Finish with a sl st and cut the yarn. Don't forget to leave enough yarn for sewing (see remaining steps). You don't need to stuff this section. Make two arms.

PROJECT

Feet Gray and white

rnd 0 = (white) Start with a magic ring.
rnd 1 = 6 sc in the ring (6 st)
rnd. 2 = 6 inc (12 st)
rnd 3-4 (2 rnds) = 12 sc
rnd 5-8 (4 rnds) = (gray) 12 sc ▶ Start stuffing.
rnd 9 = 6 dec (6 st)

Firmly stuff. Cut the yarn and, with a yarn needle, thread it through the last 6 stitches and pull tight. Don't forget to leave enough yarn for sewing (see remaining steps).
Make two feet.

Tail Gray and white

rnd 0 = (white) Start with a magic ring.
rnd 1 = 6 sc in the ring (6 st)
rnd 2 = 6 sc
rnd. 3 = *1 sc, inc* ×3 (9 st)
rnd 4 = 9 sc
rnd 5 = (gray) 9 sc ▶ Start stuffing.
rnd 6 = 1 sc, inc, *2 sc, inc* ×2, 1 sc (12 st)
rnd 7-20 (14 rnds) = 12 sc

Firmly stuff. Finish with a sl st and cut the yarn. Don't forget to leave enough yarn for sewing (see remaining steps).

Bowtie Blue

rnd 0 = Begin by chaining 18. Bring your chain into a circle by make 1 sc in the first stitch, then work 17 sc in the round (18 st).
rnd 1-2 (2 rnds) = 18 sc

Finish with a sl st and cut the yarn, leaving about 8″ (20cm) to create the bow. Flatten the ring and wrap the yarn around its middle to give it its shape. Tie a knot behind the bow and work the yarn in. Then make a chain long enough to go around the amigurumi's neck, threading it through the wrapped yarn to hold the bow on.

I crochet an amigurumi cat

REMAINING STEPS

Head/Ear Assembly: The ears should be attached between rounds 3 and 8 on each side of the head (symmetrically).

Head/Body Assembly: You should have left enough thread when finishing the head to sew it onto the body. Simply position the head over the opening of the body (use it to finish your stuffing) and sew. Then tie the bowtie around the neck.

Arms/Body Assembly: The arms are attached on each side of the body at round 26.

Feet/Body Assembly: The feet are attached under the body with their inner edge at round 3. Pay careful attention to its balance.

Tail/Body Assembly: The tail is attached behind the body at round 5. Add a stitch in round 13 to keep it aloft. Pay careful attention to its balance.

Some HELPFUL TIPS

You have just spent 21 days getting to know the art of crochet. You can now embark on many new projects! Here are some extra tips if you would like to try your hand at making clothing or even your own creations.

BLOCKING

Openwork projects will often require blocking (See Day 12 and Shawl). This allows you to give them the desired shape, but also to correctly reveal the stitching. To do this, it's helpful to have ball-head pins (often used in sewing) and a surface into which you can stick those pins (gym mat, any mat that doesn't mind getting wet, ironing board, plank, etc.).

- Make a bath of tepid water (the water must not be cold because this can damage certain materials) and submerge your work.
- Allow it to soak for several minutes before pulling it out. Absolutely do not wring out your work; lay it out on a towel then roll it up. This will get the water out without damaging the stitches.
- Then lay your work out on a large enough surface, stretching it and holding it in place with pins.

My Advice
If it's an article of clothing, use detergent that is specifically intended for delicate clothing and does not require rinsing.

Here are the examples of the granny square pouch and the shawl.

CLOTHING AND GAUGE SWATCHES

So you want to make some clothes? Then you must complete the essential step of making a gauge swatch.

This may seem like a lot of extra time, but it's very important. Even if you get the exact same yarn and the exact same hook that the pattern recommends, yarn tension and gauge make a big difference—as you may have already noticed over the course of the last 21 days. It may not be incredibly important when making an amigurumi or even a shawl, but it gains a lot of significance when making vests or sweaters. In these cases, you need to be able to trust the pattern is telling you.

Gauge swatches are often made using the same stitches as the work itself, so single crochets, double crochets, etc. If it says: 19 stitches for 26 rows, you need to start by chaining 19 and then make 26 rows.

ADVICE

> **My Advice**
> As you may have already noticed, the edges of a crocheted piece are not very flat and sometimes pucker. Don't hesitate to add 6 stitches to each row as well as two or three additional rows for your swatch, so you can properly measure the gauge in the middle of the swatch.

It is **absolutely** necessary to block the swatch before checking it, as some yarns will change in the wash. It would certainly be a pity to crochet a beautiful size M sweater only to have it become size XL after the first wash!

- If, with your gauge swatch, you achieve exactly what the pattern indicates, you can move right ahead.
- If you get more stitches than what is indicated, it's because your stitches are too small. You should switch to a larger hook.
- If you get fewer stitches, you should switch to a smaller hook and redo the swatch to make sure.

> **My Advice**
> If you want to make your own creation and it requires an exact size, make a swatch first to avoid any unpleasant surprises!

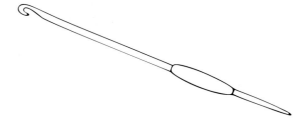

Some helpful tips — Day 21

In this picture, I have 21 stitches per 10cm (approx. 4˝). I measured the middle of the swatch to avoid the stitches on the ends.

Your mission!

You have just completed your 21 days of learning!
You can now leap right in to any project you'd like. Have fun and don't limit yourself, because remember: we learn the most from the mistakes we make!

Happy crocheting!

Crafty courses to become an expert maker...

From their studio to yours, Creative Spark instructors are teaching you how to create and become a master of your craft. So not only do you get a look inside their creative space, you also get to be a part of engaging courses that would typically be a one or multi-day workshop from the comfort of your home.

Creative Spark is not your one-size-fits-all online learning experience. We welcome you to be who you are, share, create, and belong.

Scan for a gift from us!

creativespark.ctpub.com